KT-430-071

The Official HEART OF MIDLOTHIAN 2007 Annual

"THE HEART AND SOUL OF EDINBURGH"

Written by Final Whistle Media
Roddy Mackenzie/Adriana Wright
www.finalwhistlemedia.co.uk
Acknowledgements: Michael Mackenzie

A Grange Publication

© 2006. Published by Grange Communications Ltd., Edinburgh, under licence from Heart of Midlothian Football Club. Printed in the EU.

ISBN 1-905426-23-2

£6.99

HEART OF MIDLOTHIAN FOOTBALL CLUB

Contents

INTRODUCTION

Welcome to the second full-colour official Hearts annual. After one of the most dramatic and memorable seasons in the club's history, relive the triumphs of the 2005-06 campaign which saw Hearts recapture the Scottish Cup and book a Champions League place.

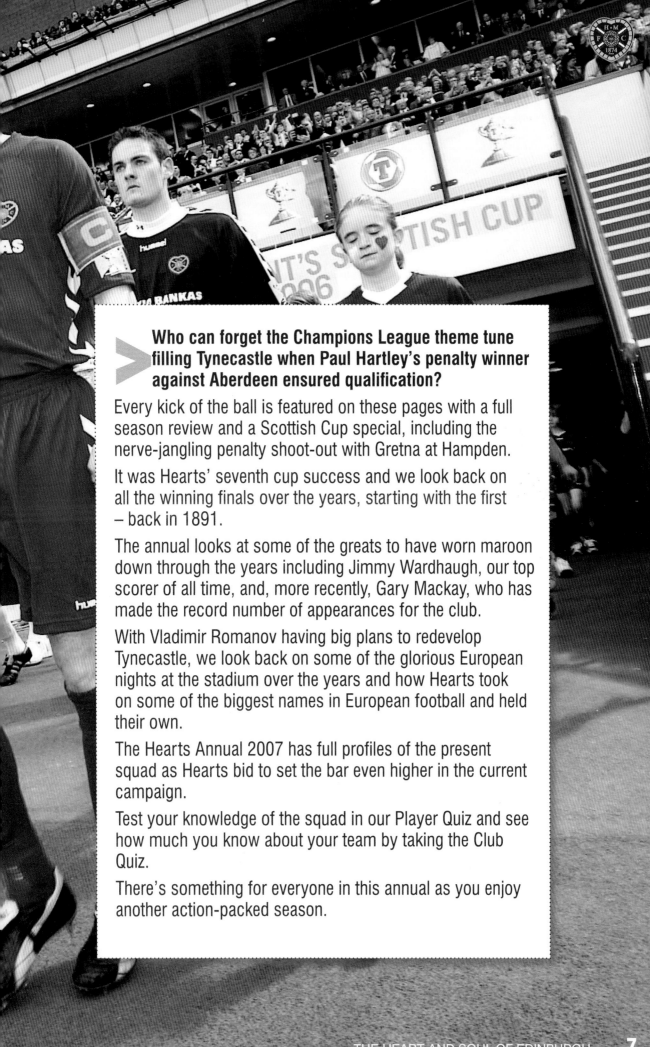

> **Who can forget the Champions League theme tune filling Tynecastle when Paul Hartley's penalty winner against Aberdeen ensured qualification?**

Every kick of the ball is featured on these pages with a full season review and a Scottish Cup special, including the nerve-jangling penalty shoot-out with Gretna at Hampden.

It was Hearts' seventh cup success and we look back on all the winning finals over the years, starting with the first – back in 1891.

The annual looks at some of the greats to have worn maroon down through the years including Jimmy Wardhaugh, our top scorer of all time, and, more recently, Gary Mackay, who has made the record number of appearances for the club.

With Vladimir Romanov having big plans to redevelop Tynecastle, we look back on some of the glorious European nights at the stadium over the years and how Hearts took on some of the biggest names in European football and held their own.

The Hearts Annual 2007 has full profiles of the present squad as Hearts bid to set the bar even higher in the current campaign.

Test your knowledge of the squad in our Player Quiz and see how much you know about your team by taking the Club Quiz.

There's something for everyone in this annual as you enjoy another action-packed season.

GOALKEEPING GREATS

> CRAIG GORDON IS FOLLOWING A LONG LINE OF GREAT GOALKEEPERS WHO HAVE GRACED TYNECASTLE AND BEYOND. HERE WE LOOK AT SOME OF THE PLAYERS WHO HAVE MADE UP HEARTS' LAST LINE OF DEFENCE OVER THE YEARS.

Jack Harkness

Played over 400 matches for Hearts, he had also represented Scotland at all levels before he was 20.

Born in Glasgow in 1907, he started out with amateur side Queen's Park before signing for Hearts in May, 1928. He spent eight years at the club during which time he won 12 international caps – the best by a Hearts' goalkeeper until Craig Gordon arrived on the scene.

Jack was also one of the famous "Wembley Wizards" side that beat England 5-1 in London.

Sadly he was forced to retire from the game prematurely at the age of 30 due to a serious leg injury, but he went on to become a sports journalist.

Gordon Marshall

Gordon Marshall made his Hearts' debut at the age of 17 as then-manager Tommy Walker showed he had complete faith in his ability.

In only his second season between the sticks, Hearts won the league title by an astonishing 13-point margin in 1958. It was a season where Hearts were noted for their goalscoring but Marshall kept an impressive 13 clean sheets in his 31 matches.

He won the the title again a couple of years later and added to his medal haul by playing in three successful League Cup final teams.

Marshall played in Hearts' first-ever European tie – against Standard Liege - when he was on the wrong end of a 5-1 scoreline.

After seven years at Tynecastle he went on to have spells at Hibs and Celtic.

Sons Scott and Gordon junior both followed him into professional football.

Henry Smith

Bought for just £2,000, Smith proved one of the Tynecastle bargain buys as he went on to play over 700 times for the club and win three Scotland international caps.

In 15 years at the club he set the record for the most number of shut-outs by a Hearts' goalkeeper (171).

Starting out in the first division with the club, he blossomed under Alex MacDonald and played a big part in the Hearts' revival in fortunes.

Commanding in his area and a terrific shot-stopper, he enjoyed a run of 180 successive matches up to February, 1991, when he was dropped after a Scottish Cup exit at Airdrie by then-manager Joe Jordan.

Fought hard to win his place back and the following year was rewarded with his first Scotland call-up against Canada. Left the club in the mid-1990s.

Gilles Rousset

The 6'5" French goalkeeper became a cult figure at Tynecastle after being brought to the club from Rennes by Jim Jefferies.

As a full international for his country, his signing was a considerable coup for the club and he did not disappoint.

A gentle giant off the field, Rousset was fiercely competitive on it and his enthusiasm for the game was infectious.

He helped Hearts to the Scottish Cup final in 1996 but made an uncharacteristic error to allow Brian Laudrup to score a killer goal in the 5-1 defeat.

But within two years, he made amends with a superb display as Hearts beat Rangers 2-1 to win their first silverware for 36 years.

Also played in a League Cup final during his time at Tynecastle, his contribution to a club that was on the rise cannot be over-estimated.

Antti Niemi

Antti Niemi was something of a surprise signing by Jim Jefferies in 1999 as he had failed to make the grade at Rangers and had spent some time on loan at Charlton.

But he went on to quickly establish himself as the Hearts' number one and one of the finest goalkeepers in Britain.

Starting out with Veikkausliiga in his native Finland, he had five years with HJK Helsinki before arriving at Ibrox in 1997.

Capable of pulling off the spectacular save, Niemi became a firm favourite at Tynecastle before moving to join Southampton in 2002.

Regarded as the best goalkeeper Finland have produced, he gave up international football after a decade in 1995. After leaving Southampton, he joined Fulham and continues to enhance his reputation in the Premiership.

Season Review

2005-06

JULY

Kilmarnock 2 Heart of Midlothian 4

> Hearts came from behind to beat Kilmarnock 4-2 in George Burley's first competitive game in charge, with debut goals from Roman Bednar and Rudolf Skacel.

Kilmarnock took the lead through Steven Naismith but Hearts equalised within a minute after the three new boys Bednar, Skacel and Edgaras Jankauskas combined for the goal scored by Skacel.

A minute into the second half Bednar's header went in off the upright before Saulius Mikoliunas rifled a beautiful 25-yarder into the far corner in the 61st minute.

Gordon Greer's 74th minute header brought Killie back into the game but their hopes of a home comeback were short lived as Jankauskas was upended in the penalty area and Paul Hartley stepped up to smash the ball into the net.

AUGUST

Heart of Midlothian 4
Hibernian 0

> Hearts moved to the top of the SPL as George Burley made capital gains in his first Edinburgh derby.

The Hearts manager saw Rudi Skacel, Paul Hartley (penalty), substitute Stephen Simmons and Saulius Mikoliunas give his side a convincing victory at Tynecastle.

Hearts took the lead after 13 minutes as Skacel bundled the ball past Zibi Malkowski. Hartley made it 2-0 in the 58th minute after Stephen Glass handled in the penalty area giving Hearts a penalty.

A mistake by Guillaume Beuzelin gave Hearts their third with substitute Simmons providing the finish.

With seven minutes left, Mikoliunas capped the win with a terrific 20-yard strike.

Dundee United 0
Heart of Midlothian 3

Hearts signalled their intentions of being serious title challengers notching up their third successive win in a 3-0 victory at Tannadice.

The visitors grabbed the lead in the sixth minute when Julien Brellier's curling free-kick allowed captain Steven Pressley to guide the ball into the net from eight yards.

Six minutes later a poor header from Grant Brebner fell to Paul Hartley, who lobbed the ball back in for Roman Bednar to turn and smack a low drive past the stranded Derek Stillie.

Rudi Skacel had the final say scoring Hearts' third in injury time to seal an impressive victory.

Heart of Midlothian 2
Aberdeen 0

The SPL leaders kept up their 100 per cent record thanks to goals from Rudi Skacel and Michal Pospisil.

Hearts grabbed the lead midway through the first half as Skacel pounced on a loose ball to draw Ryan Esson before slotting the ball into the corner of the net.

Jamie McAllister hit the post for Hearts late on with a volley before Pospisil put the result beyond doubt by firing a second into the roof of the net with five minutes left.

Heart of Midlothian 2
Motherwell 1

Hearts went five points clear at the top of the league with their fifth consecutive win but it took a breathtaking save from Craig Gordon in the dying seconds to maintain Hearts' 100 per cent record.

Rudi Skacel's scored his fifth goal in five league games as he fired Hearts ahead five minutes before the interval.

Hearts were well in control as Takis Fyssas burst down the left on 70 minutes cutting the ball back to Edgaras Jankauskas who turned it high into the net.

Motherwell pulled one back when Julien Brellier was penalised for a tug on Jim Hamilton and substitute Richie Foran slammed home the spot-kick.

This galvanised Motherwell and Hamilton missed a glorious chance before Gordon produced a fantastic late save from David Clarkson.

SEPTEMBER

Livingston 1
Heart of Midlothian 4

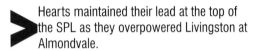

Hearts maintained their lead at the top of the SPL as they overpowered Livingston at Almondvale.

Rudi Skacel opened the scoring after ten minutes when he headed the ball home from close range. Andy Webster headed the second goal after 27 minutes when he was unmarked at a free kick.

Seven minutes later, Hartley beat the offside trap as he chased a pass from Roman Bednar before finding the net.

A minute from the break, Craig Gordon beat out a Neil Barrett free kick but Paul Dalglish tucked in the loose ball for Livi.

Any hope Livingston had of pulling it back evaporated after 62 minutes when Hartley stroked home a penalty to complete the scoring.

Inverness Caledonian Thistle 0
Heart of Midlothian 1

The Hearts' machine kept rolling on when the SPL leaders left with all three points from Inverness.

Rudi Skacel maintained his amazing goal run by firing the Jambos into the lead in the first half to make it seven goals in seven games.

Chances were few and far between in the second half, with Caley Thistle defenders working hard. In the latter stages the Highlanders had a real go, and a couple of corners caused panic in the box.

However, George Burley's high flyers made it seven straight wins to stay ahead of the pack.

Heart of Midlothian 1
Rangers 0

Hearts saw off the challenge of champions Rangers with Roman Bednar scoring the only goal of the game that secured the Tynecastle club's first home win against the Light Blues since August 1998.

The only goal of the match came after 14 minutes when Paul Hartley swung in a corner and Bednar rose completely unmarked in the box to blast a header into the corner of Ronald Wattereus' net.

Thomas Buffel came close for Rangers in the closing minutes but Hearts hung on for an important victory.

OCTOBER

Falkirk 2 Heart of Midlothian 2

▶ George Burley's side kept their unbeaten record alive in difficult circumstances as Craig Gordon was sent off midway through the first half for a challenge on Darryl Duffy who sent the resulting penalty past stand-in keeper Steve Banks.

Hearts' woes continued when Falkirk scored their second in the 67th minute as Duffy's shot rebounded off Pressley's knee and trundled over the line.

Four minutes later however the league leaders rekindled some hope when Pressley directed a Paul Hartley free-kick into the net and he saved a point for Hearts, knocking in the rebound from Deividas Cesnauskis' shot in the closing minutes.

Celtic 1
Heart of Midlothian 1

Hearts further established their credentials as title contenders as they held Celtic to a 1-1 draw at Celtic Park in a game that lived up to all of its pre-match hype and kept Hearts at the top of the table.

Celtic took the lead against the run of play when Chris Sutton's quickly taken free-kick fell to Craig Beattie who lashed his shot into the roof of the net.

But Hearts were soon level as Rudi Skacel beat Paul Telfer to the ball and from the rebound beat Boruc to send his shot into the unguarded net.

Both teams had chances to win the game, a combination of some brilliant saves and poor finishing meant the match ended in stalemate.

Heart of Midlothian 2
Dunfermline Athletic 0

Hearts produced another impressive display to open a six-point lead at the top of the SPL despite the departure of manager George Burley from the club less than 24 hours earlier.

The team showed it was business as usual scoring two goals in two minutes midway through the first half.

Rudi Skacel's low left-footer from 20 yards was gave Hearts the lead before Michal Pospisil topped it with a neat turn and subtle finish to make it 2-0.

A last-minute sending off of Pressley for a foul on Darren Young took some of the gloss off the victory.

Heart of Midlothian 1
Kilmarnock 0

Hearts maintained their three-point lead at the top of the SPL thanks to a first-half Edgaras Jankauskas strike.

Jankauskas' goal came from a great diagonal ball by Rudi Skacel that cut out the defence and left the big Lithuanian to side-foot past the on-rushing keeper on 35 minutes.

In truth though, the game never really came alive with too many niggling fouls to allow for a flowing encounter with Kilmarnock the main perpetrators.

Twice Jamie McAllister tried low shots from the edge of the box but twice Graham Smith in the Killie goal denied him.

Hibernian 2
Heart of Midlothian 0

Hearts' long unbeaten run finally ended in their 13th league game of the season as they lost 2-0 to Edinburgh rivals Hibs at Easter Road.

A red card for striker Edgaras Jankauskas left the visitors vulnerable, and two late goals from Guillaume Beuzelin and Garry O'Connor gave Hibs revenge for their 4-0 derby defeat back in August.

Paul Hartley missed an excellent opportunity early in the second half following a clever reverse pass from Skacel. But the departure of Jankauskas when he picked up his second yellow card for a push on Scott Brown killed off any hopes that Hearts had of taking more than a single point.

NOVEMBER

Heart of Midlothian 3
Dundee United 0

> Following their disappointing derby defeat Hearts got back on track with an emphatic 3-0 home victory over Dundee Utd that put them back on top of the SPL.

Paul Hartley gave Hearts them a dream start after only three minutes firing in a Saulius Mikoliunas cross from the edge of the box.

Hearts increased their lead after 25 minutes when Rudi Skacel's free-kick drifted beyond visiting keeper Derek Stillie to land inside his right-hand post.

Hearts added to their goal tally in the 57th minute as Hartley charged down Alan Archibald's clearance before cutting the ball back for Michel Pospisil to bundle the ball home from close range.

Aberdeen 1
Heart of Midlothian 1

Graham Rix took charge of his first match as Hearts boss and watched his side battle to a 1-1 draw against Aberdeen.

Aberdeen were rewarded for their positive play on 13 minutes as the Hearts defence failed to clear a cross from the right allowing Jamie Smith to drive in a shot that gave Craig Gordon no chance.

Hearts battled back brilliantly after going behind and got an unlikely equaliser on 63 minutes when a Skacel shot from 24 yards took a wicked deflection off Diamond to loop over Ryan Esson and into the net.

Motherwell 1
Heart of Midlothian 1

Hearts were forced to show their battling qualities again as they came from behind to pick up a point in a 1-1 draw against Motherwell at First Park.

Terry Butcher's men took the lead in the first half when Brian Kerr slipped the ball to the left of Hearts defensive wall which found its way to the back post where Brian McLean turned the ball into the net from close range.

Hearts bombarded 'Well for much of the second half but their pressure didn't pay off until the dying stages when Andy Webster was brought down in the box and Paul Hartley dispatched the penalty low past Smith.

CLUB QUIZ

HOW MUCH DO YOU KNOW ABOUT YOUR CLUB? TEST YOUR KNOWLEDGE WITH OUR 20-QUESTION QUIZ AND SEE HOW YOU RATE.

History

1. When was the club founded?
2. How many times have Hearts been crowned champions of Scotland?
3. What was the club's record victory?
4. When did Hearts last win the League Cup?
5. What were Hearts' original colours?

Hearts Greats

1. Which player holds the record for the most goals scored in a league campaign?
2. Who has made the most league appearances in a Hearts' shirt?
3. Who is Hearts' top all-time scorer?
4. How many caps did "King of Hearts" Willie Bauld win for Scotland?
5. Who was Hearts' first captain?

Answers on Page 61

Managers

1. Who was Hearts' manager when Wallace Mercer took control of the club in 1981?
2. Who was the last manager to take the club to the Scottish League title?
3. Which manager signed the "Terrible Trio" of Alfie Conn, Jimmy Wardhaugh and Willie Bauld?
4. Who took over the managerial reins from Alex MacDonald?
5. Who were the first Scottish League club that Jim Jefferies managed?

Europe

1. Who were Hearts' first opponents in Europe?
2. Hearts destroyed Lokomotiv Leipzig in the Cup-Winners' Cup in the first round in 1976 but which German team knocked them out in the next round?
3. Who scored Hearts' match-winner against Bayern Munich in the UEFA Cup at Tynecastle in 1989?
4. Hearts returned to European competition after an eight-year absence in 1984 but who were their opponents?
5. Who were the first team to beat Hearts in European competition at Tynecastle?

DECEMBER

Heart of Midlothian 2
Livingston 1

> A brilliant double from Rudi Skacel fired Hearts back to the top of the league and gave head coach Graham Rix his first Hearts win.

Skacel left three Livingston defenders trailing in his wake before firing a vicious 20-yarder into the top corner of Ludovic Roy's net to make it 1-0.

The visitors had barely had the chance to regroup when he added a second firing into the bottom corner of the net.

Livingston grabbed a lifeline after 63 minutes with a spectacular long-range goal from Alan Walker but held on to take the victory.

Heart of Midlothian 0
Inverness Caledonian Thistle 0

Hearts slipped four points behind league leaders Celtic as they battled out a goalless draw with a tenacious Inverness side at Tynecastle.

Hearts' best chance of the first half fell to Deividas Cesnauskis when he exchanged a one-two with Hartley but then mis-kicked in front of an open goal.

The home fans became more frustrated but Inverness continued to dominate and Craig Gordon pulled off a fine save to keep out Black's 25-yarder.

The Scotland international keeper was also at his best to tip-over a spectacular long-range effort from Brewster.

Rangers 1
Heart of Midlothian 0

A Peter Lovenkrands goal gave Rangers a 1-0 victory over Hearts at Ibrox as Graham Rix suffered his first defeat in charge.

The home side nearly took the lead when Hamed Namouchi met Robert Malcolm's free kick, but Craig Gordon superbly touched his header over.

Rangers took the lead in the second half when Namouchi's header was partially cleared but fell to Lovenkrands, who prodded the ball home at the near post.

There was further misery for Hearts when Saulius Mikoliunas was red-carded near the end.

Heart of Midlothian 5
Falkirk 0

The unbeaten run at home was stretched to 10 matches as 10-man Falkirk were crushed 5-0 at Tynecastle.

Paul Hartley made it 1-0 when he came out on top in a goalmouth scramble and slotted his right-footed shot into the net from close range.

Stephen O'Donnell piled the pressure on Falkirk when he was sent off after picking up a second yellow card and three minutes later Hearts made their one-man advantage tell as they doubled their lead through Rudi Skacel. Calum Elliot scored his first goal for Hearts four minutes before the interval to make it 3-0.

Substitute Michal Pospisil continued the rout on 73 minutes with a diving header and Elliot completed a memorable day by scoring his second in injury-time.

Heart of Midlothian 2
Celtic 3

Hearts' hopes of keeping their title dreams alive with a New Year's Day win over leaders Celtic were shattered in the dying seconds as Gordon Strachan's men fought back from 2-0 down.

The Jambos took the lead on six minutes through Edgaras Jankauskas and two minutes later captain Steven Pressley's header made it 2-0.

But Celtic substitute Stephen Pearson scored to bring Celtic right back into the game.

And when the hosts were reduced to ten men with the dismissal of Takis Fyssas it came as no surprise when Stephen McManus equalised for the visitors. Two minutes later McManus ruined Hearts' afternoon when he scored the winner.

Dunfermline Athletic 1
Heart of Midlothian 4

Stand-in striker Michal Pospisil netted a double as Hearts beat Dunfermline in the league for the third time this season.

As soon as Hearts skipper Pressley bundled Calum Elliot's mis-hit shot over the line just before the half-hour there only looked one winner. Pospisil added the second with a super finish from Robbie Neilson's cutback and it looked as though Hearts were home and dry.

But Mark Burchill had other ideas as he latched on to Ian Campbell's long free kick to fire home a lifeline for Dunfermline.

However, Pospisil put the game beyond doubt when he headed Paul Hartley's free-kick past Allan McGregor and Rudi Skacel rounded off the win with a cool finish.

Kilmarnock 1
Heart of Midlothian 0

Kilmarnock dented Hearts' title hopes with a hard-earned victory in a fiery match thanks to Danny Invincibile's strike immediately after half-time.

Rugby Park saw a rare goalless first half where Hearts had gone closest to scoring when in-form Michal Pospisil was denied by Alan Combe's point-blank save in the 18th minute.

The first period may have been goalless but Kilmarnock were ahead within 30 seconds of the restart. Invincibile fed Colin Nish in the box and Christophe Berra blocked the striker's shot, but Invincibile was perfectly placed to fire low past Craig Gordon.

Heart of Midlothian 4
Hibernian 1

A fantastic derby performance from Hearts saw them brush aside rivals Hibs 4-1 at Tynecastle to move to within eight points of league leaders Celtic.

Paul Hartley was the architect of Hibs' downfall with a first half double to cap a superb performance. And top scorer Rudi Skacel was almost as influential as Hartley as he netted his 16th goal of the season.

Hibs' cause wasn't helped when Gary Smith elbowed Saulius Mikoliunas in an off-the-ball incident and was sent off.

Hearts capitalised on the extra player only five minutes after the break when Skacel left Steven Whittaker for dead and his cross was bundled home by young Calum Elliot.

FEBRUARY

Dundee United 1
Heart of Midlothian 1

> Hearts could not reproduce the sublime form they had shown in the Edinburgh derby and were fortunate to leave Tannadice with a point as they drew 1-1 with Dundee Utd.

The visitors should have gone ahead in the 16th minute when Ludek Straceny cut the ball back only to see Michal Pospisil completely miss the ball from three yards.

The game needed a goal and it came in the 34th minute from the Terrors with a strange header from Brebner which went in off both Takis Fyssas and Craig Gordon.

Despite putting the Dundee Utd defence under pressure Hearts could not equalise until they were rewarded with a penalty in the 82nd minute when Steven Pressley went down under Alan Archibald's challenge.

Heart of Midlothian 1
Aberdeen 2

Things went from bad to worse for Hearts as they suffered a 2-1 defeat against Aberdeen at Tynecastle throwing the future of Graham Rix into doubt.

The home side started well and young Calum Elliot flicked home his fifth goal of the season from Rudi Skacel's cutback.

After the break Aberdeen were rewarded for their efforts when Hearts skipper Steven Pressley turned Scott Severin's cross into his own net before the Dons got a touch of good fortune to grab all three points with only two minutes left when Chris Clark's shot deflected in off Paul Hartley.

MARCH

Livingston 2
Heart of Midlothian 3

> The pursuit of SPL leaders Celtic was maintained but the Jambos had to rely on a late strike by substitute Roman Bednar to beat rock-bottom Livingston.

Hearts took the lead after 17 minutes when Livingston failed to clear a Calum Elliot cross and Bruno Aguiar's shot deflected in off Richard Brittain.

Livingston stunned Hearts with an equaliser in the 59th minute when Brittain beat Gordon with free kick. But Hearts went in front again when Edgaras Jankauskas headed in.

Livingston refused to lie down and Dave Mackay volleyed in a terrific equaliser 13 minutes from time, but Bednar had the final say when he put the Edinburgh side in front again three minutes from time.

Heart of Midlothian 3
Motherwell 0

Hearts' giant Lithuanian striker Edgaras Jankauskas netted twice as the Tynecastle men produced an impressive display against Motherwell.

Hearts went ahead after just three minutes when Calum Elliot played in Rudi Skacel, and his blistering left-foot shot produced a fine block from Colin Meldrum, but Jankauskas was first to react and slammed home the rebound from six yards.

Ten minutes later Jankauskas found Deividas Cesnauskis down the right and, as Martyn Corrigan cleared his cross, Jankauskas rifled home from 18 yards.

Hearts always looked likely to increase the lead, and Cesnauskis and Skacel combined for Elliot to score midway through the second half.

Inverness Caledonian Thistle 0 Heart of Midlothian 0

Hearts did themselves no favours in the race for second place in the SPL as they were held to a 0-0 draw by Inverness Caley Thistle that allowed chasing Rangers to move closer to their target.

Rudi Skacel, Edgaras Jankauskas and skipper Steven Pressley were all sidelined for the Jambos, who did at least have midfield ace Paul Hartley back in the side.

Roman Bednar was looking in fine form for the visitors and his 29th minute shot after another Richard Hastings error ended when Mark Brown dived and held the low effort.

Heart of Midlothian 1 Rangers 1

Hearts kept themselves in pole position to qualify for the Champions League as a 1-1 draw against rivals Rangers kept their lead over the third-place side to a handy six points.

In the 10th-minute some super skill from Deividas Cesnauskis took out two defenders and freed Paul Hartley, who squared the ball for Edgaras Jankauskas to side-foot home from close range.

Craig Gordon pulled off a wonder save from Thomas Buffel in the 55th minute after a free-kick was deflected into his path. But ten minutes later Buffel finally got the better of him when he arrived at the back post to squeeze an inch-perfect Burke cross into the net.

Falkirk 1 Heart of Midlothian 2

A goal from Edgaras Jankauskas with only nine minutes left gave Hearts a valuable three points away from home.

Rudi Skacel set up the opener for Hearts as he played over a low cross from the left, and Paul Hartley rushed in to bundle the ball past Mark Howard from close in.

Falkirk equalised on the stroke of half-time when Alan Gow's 20-yard free-kick struck a hand in the Hearts' wall and the referee pointed to the spot. Craig Gordon saved Gow's initial spot-kick, but the striker followed up and lashed home the rebound.

Hearts snatched the win when Tiago Rodrigues needlessly gave away possession and Calum Elliot picked out Jankauskas, whose deflected shot beat Howard.

APRIL

Celtic 1 Heart of Midlothian 0

Hearts travelled to Champions Celtic but their hopes of causing an upset evaporated as they lost 1-0 thanks to an early John Hartson strike. There seemed little threat when Maciej Zurawski found Hartson 25 yards out but his first-time volley caught Craig Gordon off balance and it bounced past the keeper and just inside the post.

Hearts were unlucky when Andy Webster saw his goal ruled out for offside early in the second half and they might have had a penalty when Bobo Balde kicked Roman Bednar.

Heart of Midlothian 4 Dunfermline Athletic 0

With Champions League rivals Rangers just three points behind in the league Hearts needed a win and produced the goods with an emphatic 4-0 victory over Dunfermline.

The Pars defence was breached in the sixth minute when Robbie Neilson launched a throw-in to the back of the six-yard box which Michal Pospisil glanced into the back of the net.

Minutes later Paul Hartley swung a crisp cross into the box for Roman Bednar to meet with a looping header to make it 2-0.

The third came when Mikoliunas drove in a 25-yard shot that went through a ruck of defenders and under keeper McGregor before substitute Juho Makela scored his first goal for the club with a six-yard effort.

Heart of Midlothian 2 Kilmarnock 0

A controversial refereeing decision and a classic Paul Hartley free kick helped Hearts to a 2-0 win over Kilmarnock that moved them five points clear of Rangers.

It could have been a different if Hearts' defender Christophe Berra had been penalised for tripping Kilmarnock striker Danny Invincibile shortly before half time.

But Berra and Hearts were spared by referee Eddie Smith, and although the visitors played strongly for much of the second period Hartley broke the deadlock with 20 minutes left with a trademark curling free-kick from 22 yards to put Hearts ahead. That man Berra added a second goal with a late header.

Hibernian 2 Heart of Midlothian 1

For the second time in the season Hearts came off second best in the Edinburgh derby as Hibs' young Moroccan signing Abdessalam Benjelloun made an instant name for himself with the winner in his first outing against Hearts.

Craig Gordon was helpless when Hibs grabbed the lead after 15 minutes as Derek Riordan's powerful half volley blasted past him.

But Hearts equalised a minute before the interval when Roman Bednar took advantage of a defensive mix-up to finish from eight yards.

Hearts were often the better side in the second half but Benjelloun's opportunistic finish 12 minutes from time was enough to give Hibs all three points.

Heart of Midlothian 3 Celtic 0

Hearts took another step closer to Champions League football next season as they beat Celtic 3-0 at Tynecastle.

Two goals in three minutes, including a Stephen McManus own goal, gave Hearts an early boost with Roman Bednar sealing the win midway through the second half.

McManus found the back of his own net in the early minutes when Paul Hartley blasted a shot at the Celtic goal and he headed past Artur Boruc while trying to clear his lines.

Hartley did claimed his 16th of the season, on nine minutes with a quickly taken free kick which caught the Celtic defence on the hop.

The result was put beyond doubt on 63 minutes when Bednar put an expert finish on a Hartley cross to make it 3-0.

MAY

Heart of Midlothian 1 Aberdeen 0

> Heart's 1-0 victory over Aberdeen sparked wild celebrations at Tynecastle as the club sealed a place in the Champions League for the first time in its history.

Paul Hartley's 54th-minute penalty, after Russell Anderson handled the ball on the goal line, was enough to settle an untidy encounter.

Aberdeen were reduced to ten men 11 minutes from time when Scott Severin was given a red card for a foul on Bruno Aguiar.

Hearts had chances to add to their lead and Jamie Langfield produced the save of the match to deny Deividas Cesnauskis. But one goal was to prove sufficient to send the Hearts fans home happy.

Rangers 2 Heart of Midlothian 0

Hearts could not end their league campaign with a win as they lost 2-0 to Rangers at Ibrox. But with the Champions League spot already tied up the result was of little consequence to the Tynecastle men.

Rangers took the lead when the unmarked Kris Boyd headed home a Peter Lovenkrands corner at the back post nine minutes before the break.

Waterreus saved well from Pospisil and Mirsad Beslija as Hearts searched for an equaliser at the start of the second half.

But Boyd was on hand to steer home a perfect Gavin Rae cross and hand Alex McLeish as 2-0 victory in his final match as Rangers manager.

WORDSEARCH

M	E	C	Y	R	R	E	B	K	G	I
S	X	L	E	S	S	B	E	E	O	N
E	Y	E	L	S	S	E	R	P	N	X
V	F	M	T	I	N	A	R	K	C	P
L	Y	C	R	J	O	L	A	N	G	R
A	S	C	A	M	A	T	S	O	E	R
C	S	T	H	C	H	Y	R	S	L	E
N	A	S	A	C	F	D	D	L	Q	B
O	S	L	R	A	O	E	A	I	S	N
G	E	E	T	N	B	T	Y	E	S	A
Y	L	N	U	N	B	E	D	N	A	R
X	L	G	O	R	D	L	Y	P	R	E

1. GORDON	2. NEILSON	3. FYSSAS
2. PRESSLEY	5. HARTLEY	6. BEDNAR
3. TALL	8. BERRA	9. ELLIOT
4. MCCANN	11. GONCALVES	

Answers on Page 61

HEARTS GREATS

Hearts have had some great servants through the years and here we look back on some of the greatest players to have worn maroon.

Alex Young

► **Alex Young was one of the most popular players ever to have played for Hearts and gained the rare distinction of winning league and cup medals on both sides of the border.**

Born in Loanhead, Young signed from Newtongrange Star and made his debut in August, 1955, in a League Cup tie against Partick Thistle which Hearts won 2-1. Fittingly, he provided the winning goal.

He was to go on to make a major impact for the club and in Hearts' glory years in the late 1950s and early 1960s, he contributed some invaluable goals.

Indeed, while the "Terrible Trio" of Alfie Conn, Jimmy Wardhaugh and Willie Bauld were feted everywhere, Young also terrorised defences and he scored 23

goals in his first season at the club and played in the Scottish Cup final victory over Celtic that season.

He had the knack of scoring important goals and his 24 goals in 34 league games in 1958 included the title clincher in a match against St Mirren at Love Street.

He also scored the match-winner when Hearts won the League Cup in 1959 and finished with another league winners' medal at the end of the campaign, this time netting 23 goals throughout the campaign.

Hearts also clinched the title at Love Street that day in a thrilling 4-4 draw with St Mirren and Young scored twice.

There was uproar amongst the fans when he was later sold to Everton in a £42,000 deal that also saw team-mate George Thomson move south but he was to go on and establish himself on Merseyside.

He won a league winners' medal with the club in 1963 and played in the famous 3-2 FA Cup final win over Sheffield Wednesday in 1966.

Young was capped eight times for Scotland – winning six of those while at Tynecastle – making his debut against England in 1960 and signing off against Portugal six years later.

After leaving Everton, he played for Glentoran in Northern Ireland before returning to play briefly for Stockport County before a knee injury hastened his retirement from the game.

Dave Mackay

> Some would argue he was the greatest Hearts player ever. Dave Mackay was certainly around when silverware was being handed out. A player who never gave less than 100 per cent, he was fully committed to the Tynecastle cause from the moment he made his debut just a week short of his 19th birthday.

His emergence coincided with the most successful spell in the club's history and, in his first season (1953-54), he helped Hearts finish runners-up to Celtic in the league, their highest placing since 1938.

The following season, he helped guide Hearts to silverware in the shape of the League Cup as he became a regular as one of the most promising wing-halves in the country.

More success followed with the Scottish Cup triumph over Celtic in 1956 and Mackay went on to captain Hearts to their first league title of the century in 1957-58.

His leadership qualities were obvious from when he first broke into the Hearts' side and manager Tommy Walker recognised this as he built his team around him. At the end of the 1956-57 season, he was called up for international duty and won his first cap in a 4-1 defeat by Spain in a World Cup qualifier in the Estadio Bernabau in Madrid where he came up against such greats as Alfredo Di Stefano and Francisco Gento.

Mackay went on to win 22 caps for his country after leaving Hearts in 1959 to join Tottenham Hotspur in a £30,000 deal. His reputation grew in England and was widely regarded as one of the best in his position in Britain. Tottenham team-mate Jimmy Greaves remarked at the time that he was the club's best-ever player.

He had great all-round ability and not only was he strong in the tackle but his passing ability was exceptional and he also enjoyed getting forward to support his front players. A stomach injury meant he had to miss out on Spurs'1963 European Cup-Winners' Cup triumph.

Five years later he joined Derby County and, under Brian Clough, played his part in his team team's rise to prominence and was voted joint Footballer of the Year in England in 1972.

After his playing days were over, he went on to achieve success as a manager at Swindon, Nottingham Forest and Derby before spending time in the Middle East where he managed Kuwait and Dubai.

Currently lives in Nottingham, but is a regular visitor to Tynecastle where he is still held in such high regard.

John Cumming

> The Carluke-born player will go down in history as one of the greatest captains of the club. He won more medals in a Hearts' shirt than any other player as he was a mainstay of the team that won seven trophies between 1954-62.

He started out as a left-winger before moving to inside-left in his early years at the club but it was when he dropped back to wing-half that he produced his best form and persuaded manager Tommy Walker that he had the qualities to lead the side.

Made his debut in December 1950 in a 2-2 draw with Celtic at Parkhead and was to go on to make over 600 appearances for the club and win nine caps for Scotland.

A tough tackler, he gained the reputation for being a hard player but, remarkably, he was never once booked in his career.

Cumming prided himself on his physical fitness and worked well under John Harvey, the Tynecastle trainer at the time who took the team on gruelling pre-season trips to the sand-dunes at Gullane.

After helping Hearts to the league title in 1958 when the team scored 132 goals and cconceded only 29, he skippered the side to the title in 1960.

His last medal came in 1962 when Hearts beat Kilmarnock 1-0 in the League Cup final and, by that stage, he was combining coaching with playing.

Such was his level of fitness that he was still registered as a player after taking up coaching duties and he did make two unexpected appearances for Hearts in the 1966-67 season as injuries took their toll on the squad.

He coached under Bobby Brown for the Scotland national side and worked under four different managers at Tynecastle, Walker, Harvey, Bobby Seith and John Haggart.

After an amazing 27 years as a player and a coach, he left the club in 1976 but the esteem with which he was held by the club was such that he was offered the chance to travel back on the team bus when Hearts won the Scottish Cup in 1998, an invitation he had to decline due to other commitments that day.

Jim Cruickshank

> Jim Cruickshank made the goalkeeper's gloves his own in the 1960s and 1970s and is regarded as one of the finest to play between the sticks for the club.

During 17 years at Hearts he made 610 appearances but, unfortunately, for the goalkeeper, there were no honours during that period.

He joined a successful Hearts team in 1960 after playing as an amateur for Queen's Park and, although he made one appearance during that first season, he had to wait until the 1963-64 season before he had an extended run in the team after the departure of Gordon Marshall.

He played in all 34 league games during the 1964-65 season when Hearts were pipped for the title by Kilmarnock on the last day of the season on goal average and it was to be the closest he came to a medal.

Jim appeared in two Scottish Cup finals – against Dunfermline in 1968 and Rangers in 1976 – but was on the losing side on both occasions.

Standing just 5'10", Cruickshank was not the tallest of goalkeepers but had great spring and agility which doubtless went back to his teenage years as a schoolboy athlete when he was the schools' long jump champion.

He was capped at every level for Scotland, including amateur, before winning his first full cap in 1964 against Germany.

Had the unusual feat of making a triple penalty save from Joe Davis in an Edinburgh derby in 1967, by which stage he was already a firm favourite with the Tynecastle faithful.

Displaying incredible consistency he did not miss a league game for four years in one spell in the 1970s and number two Kenny Garland was soon to leave the club in frustration at his lack of opportunities.

In 394 league appearances, Cruickshank kept a more than respectable 102 clear sheets at a time when the club was going through some mixed fortunes after the successful period of the late 1950s and early 1960s.

Gary Mackay

> **Gary Mackay occupies a unique place in the Tynecastle tapestry. No player has managed more games in maroon – 737 in total between 1980 and 1997 – and he also holds the record for the most league games (515) for the club. It is safe to assume that neither total will be surpassed.**

Mackay realised a childhood dream when he joined the club from Salveson boys' club but even he could not have envisaged how much of an impact he would have.

A midfield player with an eye for goal, he gave his all in every match he played as he caught the eye, not just for his whole-hearted approach but as a cultured passer of the ball.

Made his debut as a 16 year-old in a League Cup tie at Ayr United, he has given his chance early along with John Robertson and Dave Bowman in a Hearts team that was struggling in the Premier League.

When Alex MacDonald took over the managerial reins, Mackay proved a trusted player and one that the side was built around.

His understanding with Robertson was to bring goals to both players and it fired Hearts to the brink of a league and cup double in 1986, only to be cruelly caught short.

A key member of Scotland's successful youth team under Andy Roxburgh, it was no surprise when he was rewarded with his first full cap for his country when Roxburgh was elevated to the position of national team coach.

He scored a memorable goal for his country on his debut as Scotland scored an unlikely 1-0 win over Bulgaria in Sofia – a result that gave the Republic of Ireland a European Championship qualifying place for 1988, thus ensuring permanent hero status across the Irish Sea.

Mackay went on to win four caps for Scotland and, at club level, was helping Hearts with some consistent football which suggested they could regain the league title under Joe Jordan.

Late in his Tynecastle career, Mackay was to play in two more cup finals – in 1996 in a 5-1 Scottish Cup final defeat by Rangers and, later in the year, a 4-3 League Cup loss to the same opposition – and there was to be no major medal to show for his 17 years at the club.

Had a spell at Airdrie under Alex MacDonald and was briefly manager of the Lanarkshire club before setting up as a football agent but is never far from Tynecastle.

HEARTS GREATS

Jimmy Wardhaugh

> Hearts' record scorer with a remarkable 376 goals in 519 matches. One-third of the "Terrible Trio" along with Willie Bauld and Alfie Conn, he signed for Hearts as a 17 year-old in 1946 and made his debut soon afterwards in a 3-2 win over Celtic where he announced his arrival with a goal.

Signed by David McLean, he played his first match alongside Conn and Bauld in October 1948 in a 6-1 win over East Fife when he was the only member of the trio not to score (Bauld 3, Conn 2).

But it was not long before he was to feature regularly at the top of the Tynecastle scoring charts. By the following season, he had weighed in with 24 goals and he scored 34 in season 1953-54 when Hearts finished runners-up in the league to Celtic.

Played his part as Hearts finally won silverware in 1954 after almost 50 years without a trophy – finding the net in the 4-2 League Cup final win over Motherwell with Bauld scoring the other three.

It was the signal for great things ahead and Wardhaugh hit another 34 league goals in 1955-56 and this time there was a Scottish Cup winners' medal to show at the end of the campaign after a 3-1 final win over Celtic.

During the title-winning season in 1958, Wardhaugh had the distinction of scoring the 120th goal of the league campaign – which beat the previous league record of 119 set by Motherwell in the 1930s (Hearts went on to amass 132).

Wardhaugh left Hearts to join Dunfermline in a £2,000 deal in 1959 after losing his place to Bobby Blackwood but he had already secured a place in Hearts' history.

He was to lose his league scoring record to John Robertson in 1997 but his scoring record in all competitions will stand the test of time.

Was capped twice by Scotland – against Hungary and Northern Ireland – and also won nine caps for the Scottish League side.

He moved into sports journalism after his career was over but died prematurely at the age of 48.

UP FOR THE CUPS

Takis Fyssas is the only Greek player to have won national cup medals in three different countries.

> The defender completed the hat-trick for Hearts against Gretna in May but here he recounts his previous cup glories in Greece and Portugal.

Takis Fyssas likes nothing better than a day in the sun. Beaming from ear to ear after hoisting the Scottish Cup at Hampden last May, he had an extra reason to celebrate.

He knew he would also command headlines back in his native Greece after a unique record in cup finals.

"Before I played in the Scottish Cup final against Gretna, I'd been involved in four cup finals in my career – two in Greece and two in Portugal," he recalls.

"The first one was for Panionios when I was just starting out. We played against Panathinaikos and we were the outsiders but we won 1-0.

"I remember I was like a crazy guy mentioning it all the time that we could win. It was an important game for me just to show that I could play in a bigger team.

"I was just 23 and the next year I signed for Panathinaikos – their president was very angry after the cup final and took two players from our team.

"The next year, we played against Olympiakos in the cup final but I did not play as I had an injury and we lost that final.

"I went on to play in two more finals in Portugal – the first one was just a few months after I joined Benfica and we played Porto in the final.

"We won 2-1 in extra-time. I scored in the second half to make it 1-1 and I think it was the best goal of my career. I have it on DVD!

"It took the game to extra-time and then Simao score the winner for us.

"We were very happy as we had not won the cup for eight years and the victory was against such a big team.

"But, in my last year in Portugal, we played the final against a lower team, Setubal, and lost 2-1 because the previous week we had clinched the championship and we had been celebrating all week."

Fyssas has become a firm favourite with Tynecastle fans and could not have been happier at the end of last season after not only winning the cup, but helping Hearts into the Champions League.

"In Greece, we only knew about Rangers and Celtic and, when I came to Hearts, they didn't say very good things about my move in Greece," he states.

"I was very angry about this and I told myself I had to prove them wrong and that I had come to a good club.

"I knew I had to play well just to prove myself. Now, the newspapers in Greece are full of reports about Hearts and they have interviews with me.

"They want to come over here and take pictures of the Greek flags in the crowd and I am very proud because in Greece, they now know about Hearts.

"I won the European Championship with Greece which was a fantastic moment in my life and my career. But qualifying for the Champions League also felt fantastic.

"You never stop trying for the best and what has happened at this club is incredible. for this.

"In my mind, I cannot live for the past. I want to live for the present and I want to stay with Hearts for many years.

"I enjoy the mentality of the football and I'm proud to be here."

IT'S A FACT

ESSENTIAL FACTS ABOUT YOUR FAVOURITE CLUB

> Hearts played matches at the Meadows, Powburn, Powderhall and Old Tynecastle before moving to their current stadium.

> A crowd of 5,500 watched Hearts beat Bolton 4-1 in 1886 in a match to open Tynecastle Stadium.

> Hearts played in the FA Cup in 1886 and were beaten 7-1 by Darwen in Lancashire. Willie Mackay has the distinction of scoring Hearts' first – and only – goal in the competition.

> Hearts turned down a request from Real Madrid to play a challenge match in Edinburgh in 1925 due to fixture congestion.

> A Rugby League exhibition match was played at Tynecastle as far back as 1911 when the club borrowed rugby goalposts from Myreside for the occasion.

> Bobby Walker – the first "superstar" to play for the club - was the first player to reach 100 league goals for the club.

> Legendary Hearts' player and manager Tommy Walker was awarded an OBE for services to the game in 1960.

> A crowd of 133,399 packed Hampden to watch the 1956 Scottish Cup final against Celtic – the biggest crowd ever to take in a Hearts' game.

> Tommy Jenkinson was the first Hearts' player to be capped by Scotland and also the first to net for his country.

> Hearts, who originally started playing in red, white and blue, changed to the familiar maroon shirts on a permanent basis in season 1877-78.

> Brothers David and George Wilson both played in Hearts' 1906 Scottish Cup wining team.

> Hearts' record defeat was 8-1 at the hands of Vale of Leven in the Scottish Cup in 1882.

> Hearts were unbeaten for 27 games in the Premier Division in 1985-86 before they lost to Dundee on the final day of the campaign as they were pipped by Celtic to the title on goal difference.

> Drew Busby scored Hearts' first goal in the Premier Division – from the penalty spot against Dundee in September 1975 at Dens Park.

> Willie Gibson scored Hearts' first hat-trick in the Premier Division – against Celtic in November 1976.

> When Hearts beat Hibs to win the Scottish Cup in 1896 it was the only occasion the cup final has been played outside of Glasgow. The match was played at Logie Green in Edinburgh, home of St Bernards.

> When Hearts beat Hibs in last season's Scottish Cup semi-final, it was only the second time the Edinburgh rivals have met at that stage in the competition. The only other occasion was in 1901 when Hearts won 2-1 after a replay at Easter Road.

> Legendary forward Jimmy Wardhaugh once scored eight goals in a match – against Burntisland Shipyard in a 12-2 win in 1952.

> The first live match to be broadcast on television from Tynecastle was the European Cup first round match with Royal Standard Liege from Belgium in 1958.

> Hearts' first all-ticket match was for a Scottish Cup match against Celtic at Tynecastle in 1939.

THE ROAD TO GLORY

Hearts were seemingly destined to lift the Scottish Cup in 2006. It came 100 years after they had beaten Third Lanark in the final and 50 years after a cup final win over Celtic at Hampden. Here, we look at the route to the latest triumph…

Third round: Hearts 2 Kilmarnock 1

The sight of Jim Jefferies back at Tynecastle on Scottish Cup business no doubt reminded Hearts of the day in 1998 when he brought the cup back to Gorgie but his well-drilled Kilmarnock team represented a difficult opening hurdle.

Hearts started well and Edgaras Jankauskas hit the post with a terrific 25-yard shot which had Alan Combe well beaten.

But Hearts struggled to find their rhythm and it was left to skipper Steven Pressley to ease concerns when he headed the opening goal after 24 minutes from a long throw-in by Robbie Neilson.

Hearts lost Jankauskas through injury a minute from the break, replaced by Michal Pospisil, and there was little to choose between the teams at half-time.

Chances were few and far between in a game which became bogged down in midfield but Hearts always looked the more likely to find the net.

Rudi Skacel and Calum Elliot both came close before the deciding moment arrived with only 15 minutes left.

It was Elliot who provided the cross for substitute Jamie McAllister to get the all-important second goal.

Kilmarnock refused to lie down and Colin Nish pulled a goal back with four minutes left to ensure an uncomfortable final few minutes for Hearts.

Team: Gordon; Neilson, Pressley, Webster, Fyssas, Mikoliunas (McAllister 70), Hartley, Brellier, Skacel (Berra 89), Elliot, Jankauskas (Pospisil 44).

Fourth round: Hearts 3 Aberdeen 0

> Hearts welcomed another home draw, albeit against another Premierleague side. But the enthusiasm was tempered by the fact that Hearts had never beaten Aberdeen at Tynecastle in the Scottish Cup and progress would mean breaking new ground.

Hearts were without the suspended Paul Hartley and Rudi Skacel and Takis Fyssas were both missing through illness.

Hearts did not start too convincingly and, if anything, Aberdeen looked the more likely to score in the early stages. But that all changed in the 21st minute when Michal Pospisil scored a breathtaking goal when he controlled a pass from Calum Elliot on his chest before rifling a 16-yard shot past Jamie Langfield.

Hearts were 2-0 up after 34 minutes when Deividas Cesnauskis set up Elliot who scored with some ease. Worse was to follow for Aberdeen when Pospisil was brought down by Zander Diamond in the penalty area. The Aberdeen defender was red-carded and Steven Pressley cracked home the penalty to give Hearts a handsome half-time advantage.

It was to prove more than sufficient and there was no way back for Aberdeen

in the second half as Hearts were content to play out the remaining 45 minutes in the knowledge that their place in the last eight was secure.

Team: Gordon; Neilson, Pressley, Webster, Beslija, Cesnauskis, Brellier (McAllister 60), Johnson, Goncalves, Elliot (Makela 52), Pospisil.

Quarter-final: Hearts 2 Partick Thistle 1

> Another home draw but this time against second division opposition, it seemed as if the gods

were smiling on Hearts. Partick, under Dick Campbell, had proved inconsistent all season but had knocked Inverness Caledonian Thistle out in the previous round after a replay and were capable of raising their game.

Any hint of a shock appeared to have evaporated as early as the sixth minute when Edgaras Jankauskas headed in a Paul Hartley cross.

But Hearts toiled to make much more of an impact after this and Partick had their moments before the end of the first half with Stephen McConalogue and Mark Roberts both going close.

But the game turned back Hearts' way within a few minutes midway through the second half. Partick thought they had equalised when a deflected free-kick from Billy Gibson seemed to wrong foot Craig Gordon but the goalkeeper somehow managed to recover to claw the ball to safety. Almost immediately, Hearts made it 2-0 when Deividas Cesnauskis scored with a fine shot into the roof of the net from the edge of the area.

But, with 12 minutes left, Roman Bednar was sent off after picking up his second yellow card and then Roberts pulled a goal back for Partick. Hearts were on the ropes in the final minutes and Darren Brady carelessly blasted over when he had a chance of taking the tie to a replay. It was a relieved Hearts who greeted the final whistle and a semi-final place.

Team: Gordon; Neilson, Pressley, Webster, Fyssas, Cesnauskis (Berra 81), Brellier, Hartley, Skacel (Mikoliunas 66), Jankauskas, Elliot (Bednar 61).

Semi-final: Hearts 4 Hibernian 0

> Paul Hartley produced his best performance in a maroon shirt to settle one of the most anticipated Edinburgh derby matches in years.

Many had hoped the semi-final draw would keep the capital pair apart with Rangers and Celtic both out of the competition and lower division Dundee and Gretna also in the hat.

But it was not to be and, after debate about the merits of holding such a game at Murrayfield, a crowd of over 43,000 packed Hampden for the Sunday clash already in the knowledge that Gretna awaited in the final.

Hibs were short-handed because of injuries but battled hard and Gary Caldwell should have done better with a header in front of goal.

But Hartley then took matters into his own hands. He exchanged passes with Edgaras Jankauskas in the 27th minute before beating Zibi Malkowski with a deft flick.

Hearts lost influential skipper Steven Pressley at half-time after he had sustained a head knock and it meant a reshuffle in the ranks.

Malkowski produced the save of the match to keep out a deflected free-kick from Hartley before the Hearts' midfield player conjured up the killer second goal direct from a free-kick after 59 minutes with Malkowski failing to cover his near post.

Hibs looked a beaten team and Ivan Sproule was red carded 13 minutes from time for stamping on Saulius Mikoliunas.

Three minutes later, Malkowski was at fault again as he failed to clear his lines and Jankauskas nipped in for a calmly-taken third goal.

In the final minute, Gary Smith was sent off after tugging Michal Pospisil in the penalty area and it left the way clear for Hartley to complete his hat-trick from the spot. Hearts had made it into their first Scottish Cup final in eight years.

Team: Gordon; Neilson, Pressley (Fyssas 45), Webster, Goncalves (Mikoliunas 69), Cesnauskis, Hartley, Aguiar, Skacel, Jankauskas, Elliot (Pospisil 82).

THE MAGNIFICENT
SEVEN

Hearts' Scottish Cup triumph over Gretna last May was the seventh time the trophy was brought back to Gorgie. Here, we look back on all the triumphs, starting with the first piece of silverware the club won – the Scottish Cup in 1891 – and ending with that magnificent seventh cup success.

○ 1891 Hearts 1 Dumbarton 0

> Hearts had to endure a marathon journey to the Hampden final, playing in no fewer than seven rounds before booking their place against Dumbarton.

In a season when Hearts hardly sparkled in the league, they found their scoring touch in the cup with 27 goals on their way to the trophy.

Hearts beat Raith Rovers 7-2 in the first round before getting a walkover in the second round against Burntisland Thistle. Hearts then beat Methlan Park 3-0 in the third round at Meggatland followed by Ayr (4-3), Morton (5-1) and East Stirling (3-1) before easing past Third Lanark 4-1 in the semi-final at Cathkin.

A crowd of 16,000 attended the final at Hampden which was played in early February. Willie Mason scored the only goal of the game after 15 minutes as Hearts saw off Dumbarton by the narrowest of margins.

◯◯ 1896 Hearts 3 Hibernian 1

> It remains the only occasion when the cup final was played outside Glasgow – an all-Edinburgh final making it common sense to play the game on a neutral ground in Edinburgh, Logie Green (home of St Bernard's).

To date, it is still the only time Hearts and Hibs have met in the final of the competition but there was widespread hope it might be repeated before last season's semi-final draw.

A solitary Willie Michael goal in the semi-final with St Bernard's put Hearts through to the final. They had progressed through the rounds with wins over Blantyre (12-1), Ayr (5-1) and Arbroath (4-0) to set up the final clash with Hibs.

A crowd of 17,000 packed into Logie Green with tickets costing one shilling (5p) each but it was Hearts who dominated the final to hoist the trophy with goals from Davie Baird, Alex King and Willie Michael.

◯◯◯ 1901 Hearts 4 Celtic 3

> Bobby Walker was tagged as Hearts' first "superstar" and certainly his fame spread across Europe as the Tynecastle club enjoyed one of their most successful periods.

The cup final went down as a classic and was remembered as the "Walker Final" as the player was at the peak of his form.

Hearts progressed to the last four that season with victories over Mossend Swifts (7-0), Queen's Park (2-1) and Port Glasgow (5-1).

Five years after the all-Edinburgh final, Hibs had their chance to take revenge when they were paired with Hearts in the semi-finals. This time there was little between the teams and, after a 1-1 draw, Hearts won the replay with goals from Walker and Willie Porteous.

It set up a final clash with Celtic at Ibrox. Hearts, who finished ninth out of ten in the league, were underdogs going into the match but skipper Walker soon changed that. He opened the scoring early in the game and Mark Bell and Charlie Thomson were also on the scoresheet as Hearts built up a 3-1 lead. But Celtic pulled a goal back to set up a frantic finish. It was up to Walker to seal the win as he struck a shot which the Celtic goalkeeper could not hold and Bell tucked in the loose ball to ensure the victory.

○○○○ 1906 Hearts 1 Third Lanark 0

> **Hearts won the Scottish Cup for a fourth time in 1906 in a season where they also finished runners-up in the league to Celtic.**

In the cup, Hearts beat Nithsdale Wanderers 4-1 and Beith 3-0 before putting out Celtic 2-1 in the quarter-finals in front of 50,000 fans in Glasgow. Port Glasgow were next to fall, 2-0 in the semi-finals and, if the final did not live up to the 1901 against Celtic, Hearts fans were celebrating the 1-0 win over Third Lanark at Ibrox.

Hearts wore light blue for the occasion and Bobby Walker was once again an influential figure in a tense final.

He set up the only goal of the game for George Wilson with just nine minutes of the game remaining when a replay looked the most likely outcome.

Hearts were now growing accustomed to trophy success but it was to be another 50 years before the Scottish Cup made the journey back to Tynecastle.

○○○○○ 1956 Hearts 3 Celtic 1

> **Hearts reached the 1956 cup final without losing a goal en route as they saw off Forfar (3-0), Stirling Albion (5-0) and Rangers (4-0) before being taken to a replay by Raith Rovers in a goalless semi-final at Easter Road before coming through 3-0.**

Around 50,000 fans made the journey to Hampden for the final against Celtic which attracted a crowd of 132,840.

Freddie Glidden captained the team and Hearts were first to settle with a goal from Ian Crawford after 20 minutes with a shot from outside the penalty area. But there was drama before half-time when John Cumming had to go off for treatment for a head injury.

Cumming emerged after half-time with his wound bandaged and his courage inspired Hearts to new heights. Crawford scored his second shortly after the break but Willie Haughney pulled a goal back for Celtic shortly afterwards.

It was left to Alfie Conn to secure the win with just ten minutes left after Willie Bauld had headed the ball into his path.

It ended Hearts' long separation from the trophy but it was to be another 42 years before the open-top bus would journey through Edinburgh again.

○○○○○○ 1998 Hearts 2 Rangers 1

► Hearts' fans were growing impatient for silverware by the time the 1998 triumph came around. It had been almost 36 years since the club had last won a trophy and there had been some heart-breaks to endure along the way.

Hearts had been humbled in the final against Rangers at Hampden two years previously but this time there was to be no repeat as manager Jim Jefferies plotted Rangers' downfall meticulously.

Hearts reached the final without having to play a Premier League side on the way, coming through against Clydebank (2-0), Albion Rovers (3-0), Ayr United (4-1) and Falkirk (3-1).

With Hampden out of commission due to reconstruction, Hearts made the journey to Celtic Park to face a Rangers team who needed a victory to avoid a trophy-less season in Walter Smith's last year in charge.

Hearts could hardly have had a better start when Sergio Porrini brought down skipper Steve Fulton in the penalty area before even a minute had elapsed. Colin Cameron kept his cool to beat Andy Goram with the penalty and Hearts then sought to defend the slender lead and hit on the break.

It worked to perfection as Lorenzo Amoruso failed to cut out a long through ball early in the second half and Stephane Adam pounced to put Hearts 2-0 ahead.

Substitute Ally McCoist pulled a goal back and goalkeeper Gilles Rousset – the fall guy in the 1996 final - was called upon to make several superb saves to ensure the cup was bound for Gorgie.

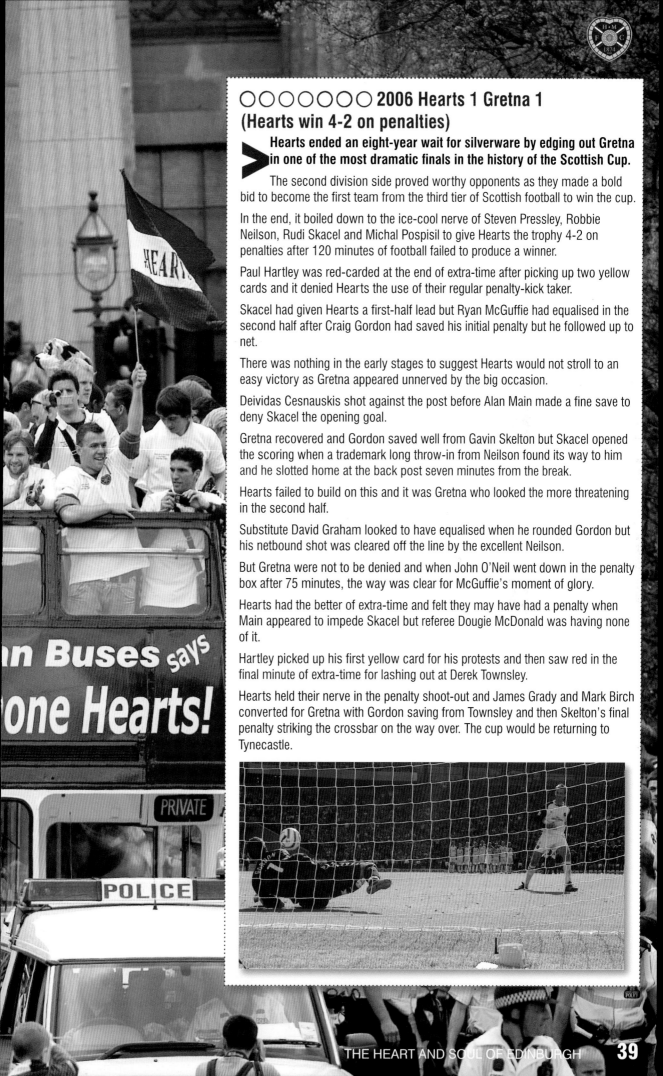

○○○○○○○ 2006 Hearts 1 Gretna 1
(Hearts win 4-2 on penalties)

▶ Hearts ended an eight-year wait for silverware by edging out Gretna in one of the most dramatic finals in the history of the Scottish Cup.

The second division side proved worthy opponents as they made a bold bid to become the first team from the third tier of Scottish football to win the cup.

In the end, it boiled down to the ice-cool nerve of Steven Pressley, Robbie Neilson, Rudi Skacel and Michal Pospisil to give Hearts the trophy 4-2 on penalties after 120 minutes of football failed to produce a winner.

Paul Hartley was red-carded at the end of extra-time after picking up two yellow cards and it denied Hearts the use of their regular penalty-kick taker.

Skacel had given Hearts a first-half lead but Ryan McGuffie had equalised in the second half after Craig Gordon had saved his initial penalty but he followed up to net.

There was nothing in the early stages to suggest Hearts would not stroll to an easy victory as Gretna appeared unnerved by the big occasion.

Deividas Cesnauskis shot against the post before Alan Main made a fine save to deny Skacel the opening goal.

Gretna recovered and Gordon saved well from Gavin Skelton but Skacel opened the scoring when a trademark long throw-in from Neilson found its way to him and he slotted home at the back post seven minutes from the break.

Hearts failed to build on this and it was Gretna who looked the more threatening in the second half.

Substitute David Graham looked to have equalised when he rounded Gordon but his netbound shot was cleared off the line by the excellent Neilson.

But Gretna were not to be denied and when John O'Neil went down in the penalty box after 75 minutes, the way was clear for McGuffie's moment of glory.

Hearts had the better of extra-time and felt they may have had a penalty when Main appeared to impede Skacel but referee Dougie McDonald was having none of it.

Hartley picked up his first yellow card for his protests and then saw red in the final minute of extra-time for lashing out at Derek Townsley.

Hearts held their nerve in the penalty shoot-out and James Grady and Mark Birch converted for Gretna with Gordon saving from Townsley and then Skelton's final penalty striking the crossbar on the way over. The cup would be returning to Tynecastle.

Hjalmar Thorarinsson
Iceland

Julien Brelier
France

Bruno Aguiar
Portugal

Jose Goncalves
Portugal

Samuel Camazzola
Brazil

Ibraham Tall
Senegal

THE WORLD

Juho Makela
Finland

Saulius Mikoliunas
Lithuania

Deividas Cesnauskas
Lithuana

Edgar Jankauskas
Lithuania

Michal Pospisil
Czech Republic

Roman Bednar
Czech Republic

Mirsa Beslija
Bosnia

Takis Fyssas
Greece

Steven Pressley

Born in Elgin on October 11, 1973, he has been the rock at the centre of the Hearts defence for the last eight seasons since he was brought to the club by Jim Jefferies in the summer of 1998 and looks set to finish his career at the Tynecastle club that he has made his own.

Steven made his football breakthrough into a star-studded first-team at Ibrox in season 1992-93 and the following season played 23 league matches as Rangers won the title.

Coventry City paid £630,000 for his service in October 1994 and he went on to play 19 matches and score once for the Sky Blues before he returned to Scotland the following summer to sign for Dundee United in a £750,000 deal.

Was a key figure for United and helped revive them to a third place SPL finish in 1997 and to the League Cup final the following season.

Pressley's commitment to the team has been unflinching over the years and he even served a spell as co-manager alongside John McGlynn following the departure of John Robertson from the club in 2005.

Won his first Scotland cap in March 2000 in a friendly match against France when he came on as a second-half substitute for Paul Ritchie and has since gone on to become an integral part of the Scotland defence playing in the impressive World Cup qualifying displays against Belarus and Slovenia last season.

Made club captain in April 2001 he featured in 29 of Hearts league matches as they battled their way into the Champions League last season.

But surely the highlight of his career so far was lifting the Scottish Cup at Hampden where Steven lived up to his 'Captain Courageous' tag as he led Hearts to victory losing a tooth in the process.

"It was a very memorable moment for me as captain of Hearts and lifting the cup. There aren't many occasions like that in your professional career," he said.

Craig Gordon

The SPL's Player of the Year in the 2005/06 season Craig played in all but two of Hearts' league matches and featured in every round of the victorious Scottish Cup run.

The big shot-stopper is also now firmly established as Scotland's number one goalkeeper making seven appearances for Walter Smith's national team last season. Berti Vogts handed him his first cap in a friendly win over Trinidad & Tobago in May, 2004, and he has never let the international team down. Recent performances include clean sheets in the World Cup qualifying matches against Belarus and Slovenia.

Born on December 31, 1982, he has been linked to the club since the age of 12 when he played for Tynecastle Boys' Club. Went on to graduate through the ranks and played with the Hearts' youth team that beat Rangers in the BP Youth Cup final and in 2000 and also played in the side that won the Scottish Youth League the following year.

Highly regarded by the Hearts' coaching staff from a young age, he was farmed out on loan to Cowdenbeath to get some first-team experience in September, 2001 before returning to Tynecastle.

His first-team debut came against Livingston in October 2002 when Antti Niemi was injured and he replaced another Finnish goalkeeper Tepi Moilanen a year later as Hearts' number one.

His save from Derek Townsley's penalty in the Scottish Cup Final against Gretna handed Hearts the coveted trophy and sums up Craig's crucial contribution to side over a historic season.

Craig has now committed his future to the club after signing a contract that ties him to the Tynecastle side until at least 2009.

Robbie Nielson

Robbie appeared in all but one of Hearts' league encounters last season bringing his tally of league appearances for the Tynecastle side to 119 over a ten-year period at the club.

Having signed back in 1996, Robbie is currently the longest-serving player at Tynecastle and is now firmly established as a first-team favourite.

Born on June 19, 1980, the dependable right-back signed from Rangers Boys Club but took several years to establish himself as a first-team regular at Tynecastle.

He was in the Hearts' youth team that won the BP Youth Cup in 1998 and, after gaining youth caps for Scotland, was called up for the Scotland Under-21 squad in spite of the fact he had not yet played first-team football for Hearts.

Loaned to Cowdenbeath between December 1999 and February 2000, he returned to Tynecastle and started 16 league games in the 2000-01 season.

Another loan spell followed in August 2002, this time to Queen of the South.

Returned in January 2003 to play five first-team games before the end of the season before making more of an impression in 2003-04 where he started 25 league games for the club.

Robbie was also instrumental in Hearts' Scottish Cup victory last season playing in every round of the competition.

Paul Hartley

Another contender for player of the year, Paul contributed 14 goals to Hearts' league campaign last season and is set to be key to their Champions League plans this season.

The former Hibs player is now firmly established as a Tynecastle favourite standing in as team captain in the absence of Steven Pressley.

Born on October 19 1976 he started his career at Hamilton Academical in 1994 before transferring to London side Millwall for £400,000. He returned to Scotland in August 1997 joining Raith Rovers who he helped to third place in the First Division before moving to Easter Road in December 1998. He was a regular in the Hibs side of 1999/2000 that finished sixth in the SPL and reached the Scottish Cup semi-final but could not settle at the Edinburgh club and joined St Johnstone.

Paul has made himself a favourite with the Hearts fans since signing from the Perth club in June 2003 consistently producing man-of-the-match performances and scoring spectacular goals.

The highlight of his season was the hat trick against former club Hibs in the semi-final of the Scottish Cup, arguably one of his most important contributions of a fantastic season.

His form has made him a regular in Walter Smith's Scotland side and he scored in the 3-0 win over Slovenia in October 2005.

Following continued speculation of a move to Celtic, Paul has committed his future to Hearts.

Ibrahim Tall

Senegalese international Ibrahim Tall found the route into the Hearts first team a difficult one after arriving at the club in August 2005 from FC Sochaux-Montbeliard in the French First Division.

Born on June 23 1981 Ibrahim is a tall defender who is equally comfortable at right-back or in the centre of defence but it took until the final weeks of the 2005/06 season for him to break into the Hearts side under manager Valdas Ivanauskas.

He began his professional career in France with CS Louhans-Cuiesaux before moving up the leagues.

A regular in the Sochaux team for three seasons, Ibrahim made over 70 appearances for the club as well as picking up international caps for Senegal, the country of his parents.

Ibrahim made just five appearances at the end of last season but made an immediate impact on the team and took part in the Scottish Cup Final.

Bruno Aguiar

Midfielder Bruno joined Hearts in January 2006 and made an almost immediate impact on the club featuring in 12 matches in his first season, including a Scottish Cup Final appearance, and scoring one goal.

Born in Lisbon on February 24 1981, Bruno began his football career at an early age joining Benfica at age nine and coming through their youth ranks.

In 2001 he went out on loan to Gil Vicente for one season before joining FC Alvera in 2002 for two season. But in 2004 he was recalled by Benfica and given a baptism of fire as he made his debut against Anderlecht in a Champions League match in August 2004. Bruno played 18 matches for Benfica that season as they won the Portuguese Championship.

Along the way Bruno has also been capped by his country at youth and Under21 level.

In December 2005 he left Benfica and moved to Lithuania's FBK Kaunas before coming to Tynecastle on loan.

Roman Bednar

A formidable presence in the box, powerful striker Roman Bednar has been garnering interest from clubs around Europe since his time with Czech Second Division side FK Mlada Boleslav in 2004.

He was brought to Hearts in the summer of 2005 by George Burley, signing on loan from FBK Kaunas in Lithuania and made an immediate impact on the club as he scored on his SPL debut against Kilmarnock on July 30th.

Born on March 26 1983 Roman began his career at CAFC Prague in his native Czech Republic before moving to the Czech First Division in 1998 with Bohemians Prague.

In 2004 he helped FK Mlada Boleslav to the Czech Second Division title and continud to impress in the league the following season. In 2005 he was voted 'Discovery of the Year' in the Czech league.

Fortunately for Hearts fans it was the Jambos who discovered him and he scored seven goals in 19 league appearances for the club in his first season.

Calum Elliot

Born in Edinburgh on March 30 1987 teenager Calum is a product of the Hearts Youth set-up and has fought his way into the first team on the back of solid performances which belie his young age.

A skilful attacker with the physical strength to match his ability Calum has been a regular feature of various Hearts youth teams for several years.

He was handed his senior debut in September 2004 against Inverness Caledonian Thistle but only went on to make a handful of appearances in his first full season.

2005/06 proved to be the breakthrough season for the striker as he made 34 first-team appearances and scored six goals including a double in the SPL match against Falkirk on Boxing Day.

Still just 19 years of age Calum looks to set to be a regular face in the Hearts line-up for many seasons to come.

Neil McCann

Veteran midfielder Neil is in his second spell with Hearts after re-signing from Southampton in January 2006.

Unfortunately his first match back in a maroon shirt against Kilmarnock in the SPL was marred by a medial ligament injury that brought the 2005/06 season to a premature end for the player.

Born in Greenock on November 8 1974 Neil started his career at Dundee before moving on to Hearts in 1996 and then Rangers two years later.

He was one of the heroes who beat Rangers 2-1 in the 1998 Scottish Cup Final to lift the trophy – the last side to do so before the current crop of players.

He joined Southampton on August 5 2003 for £1.5million but a series of injuries made it difficult for him to maintain his place in the team and he decided on a return to Scotland.

Neil has made nearly 30 appearances for the Scottish national side, his debut coming in September 1998 against Lithuania.

Julien Brellier

Frenchman Julien has quickly become a fans' favourite at Tynecastle and often has his name sung out by the crowds in Gorgie. The defensive midfielder was signed by Hearts in the summer of 2005 by then manager George Burley and made 31 appearances in his first season with the club.

Formerly with Italian giants Inter Milan, Julien is nicknamed Le Juge, or the judge, a tag that has followed him to Tynecastle where he plays just in front of the back four.

Born on January 10 1982, Julien started his career at French club Montpellier before being recruited by Inter in 2000. He made a limited number of appearances with the Serie A side and was loaned out to AC Lecce, AC Legano, Salernitana and Venezia.

He was released by Inter in 2005 and quickly snapped up by Hearts. He made his competitive debut in the 4-0 derby victory over Hibs at Tynecastle.

Michal Pospisil

Czech striker Michal Pospisil has become something of a super-sub for Hearts picking up eight goals in 29 appearances for the club, many after coming off the bench.

A strong, aggressive forward, at 6'3" he poses a major aerial threat, particularly at set-pieces.

Michal joined the club in July 2005 from Slovan Liberec where he has built up a reputation as one of the Czech Republic's most exciting strikers.

As part of the Czech side which won the European U21 Championships in 2002, he contributed the first penalty for his country as they beat France in the final shoot-out.

Michal started his career at Slavoj Zbraslav before moving to Dukla Prague and then Sparta Prague in 1992.

He played in the Champions League with Sparta before moving on to Viktoria Zizkov where he played in the UEFA Cup and won the Czech Republic Cup.

In July 2003 he moved on to Slovan Liberec where he scored 24 goals in 74 games.

After making his debut for Hearts in August 2005 against Dundee Utd he scored his first goal in the same month against Aberdeen.

Christophe Berra

A product of the Hearts youth system, 21-year-old Christophe has continued to make a valuable contribution to the Tynecastle First Team despite the appearance of many new players at the club.

Born on January 31, 1985, Christophe signed professional forms in April 2002 after impressing in the youth side.

Proving himself to be a more than able deputy when called into the team to cover for injuries, he featured in 14 matches for Hearts last season and scoring his debut goal for the club in the 2-0 league victory over Kilmarnock in April 2006.

Made his first-team debut as a substitute in a 2-1 defeat by Dundee United at Tannadice in November 2003 and started his first game, a 1-1 draw with Kilmarnock at Rugby Park, in March 2004.

International recognition followed when he was called into the Scotland Under-21 squad for the away match against Italy and he played in the 2-0 defeat.

He has the ability to play at a high level and the potential to be part of the backbone of the Hearts team for years to come.

Lee Wallace

Local lad Lee has continued to make progress and live up to his tag as a star of the future at Tynecastle making 15 appearances in the First Team last season.

The teenager has been signed up by the club until 2008 and is considered a strong prospect for the future.

He made his playing debut in the Scottish Cup Fourth Round draw against Kilmarnock on February 5 2005. Before going on to impress team mates and fans by running 70 yards to score a stunning individual goal in the replay ten days later setting Hearts on the road to victory.

Born on August 21 1987 the left-back has now made 32 first-team appearances for the club. He has found his niche on the left side of the defence forcing more experienced players out of the position.

Possessing an old head on young shoulders he has drawn comparisons with former Hearts defender and Scotland regular Gary Naysmith.

Deividas Cesnauskis

Deividas had continued to contribute to Hearts' league and Cup performances on a regular basis since joining the club in January 2005. Making regular appearances last season he scored just once.

The Lithuanian midfielder, who has earned over 20 caps for his country, started his playing days at FK Ekranas Panevezys playing in the Lithuanian Cup Final win in May 2000. He rapidly attracted attention from outside his home country and was signed up by Dynamo Moscow in 2001. He moved across the Russian capital in December 2003 to join Lokomotiv Moscow and helped them to the Russian League Championship.

Deividas was on his way back to his Lithuanian roots and FBK Kaunas when Hearts swooped in to sign him beating off strong opposition for his services from other European sides.

He could not have made a faster impact on his new club as he scored on his debut in the Scottish Cup Fourth Round replay against Kilmarnock on February 16 2005 at Rugby Park.

Saulius Mikoliunas

Saulius quickly made an impact on Scottish football when he arrived from FBK Kaunas in January 2005 and has continued to make waves over the past season contributing three goals on his regular appearances in a maroon jersey.

The player, who was born on May 2 1984, started out at Lithuanian club Sviesa Vilnius before joining FBK Kaunas in 2003. He gained a reputation as one of the country's most dangerous front men when FBK won the Lithuanian Championship in 2004.

He has become a regular in the Lithuanian international side and featured in the Champions League with FBK.

The Lithuanian international proved himself a quick and skilful winger in his debut against Livingston on January 25 2005 and scored his first goal for the club in the 3-0 win over Kilmarnock on February 12.

Edgaras Jankauskas

The Vilnius-born striker has become a firm favourite with Tynecastle fans for his direct style.

The Lithuanian international made his mark with Real Sociedad in Spain after spells in Russia with CSKA Moscow and Torpedo Moscow and Club Brugge in Belgium.

After two years in the Spanish Primera Liga he moved to Benfica in Portugal and then joined FC Porto in July 2002.

Helped Porto to the Portuguese title in his first season when they also won the UEFA Cup (although he missed the final with Celtic through injury) and, the following season, was part of the squad that won the Champions League under Jose Mourinho.

He arrived in the summer of 2005 on loan from Kaunas as one of George Burley's first recruits and did not take long to prove himself.

His presence up front ensures no defender enjoys playing against him.

Netting 12 goals last season, his tally included one in the Scottish Cup semi-final win over Hibs at Hampden.

Mirsad Besjila

Mirsad arrived at Tyncastle in January 2006 after nearly five years playing in Belgium's top flight with Racing Genk.

Born in Zivinice, Bosnia on July 6 1979, Mirsad began his career in his native country playing for NK Bosna before moving to on of Bosnia's biggest clubs, NK Zeljeznicar of Sarajevo who he helped to a Bosnian League and Cup double in the 2000/01 season.

Widely recognised as one of the paciest midfielder around Mirsad joined up with Racing Genk in July 2001 and went on to establish himself as a first-team regular and a fans favourite playing 133 matches and scoring 16 goals for the team. At the same time he picked up nearly 40 international caps representing Bosnia.

Mirsad made just five appearances for the club in his first season but has signed a three-and-a-half-year deal to play for Hearts keeping him at Tynecastle until 2009 so has plenty of time to establish himself in Valdas Ivanauskas' line-up.

Jose Goncalves

Defender Jose was born in Portugal on September 17 1985 but raised in Switzerland where he moved at the age of two with his parents. He began playing football at FC Basel where he came through the youth set up but got his professional debut in 2004 when he was signed up by Swiss Challenge League club FC Winterthur.

In January 2005 Jose moved to Italian Serie B club AC Venezia but made just three appearances but months later returned to Switzerland where he was signed by FC Thun.

Whilo at Thun he played in the Champions League eight times including matches against European giants such as Arsenal and Ajax.

FBK Kaunas beat off interest from several English clubs to sign Jose in January 2006 and soon after he moved to Tynecastle on a loan deal.

Mauricio Pinilla

Chilean striker Mauricio has played football all over Europe and has valuable Champions League experience that could help Hearts on their European campaign this season.

Signed by Valdas Ivanauskas on loan from Sporting Lisbon for one year in July 2006 after impressing in a trial Mauricio is hoping to find the back of the net as often as possible.

Born on February 4 1984 the 22-year-old began his career in his native Santiago making his professional debut in 2002 for Universidad de Chile.

He remained there for just one year before moving to Italy where he played for both Chievo and Inter Milan.

A move to the Spanish League and Celta Vigo followed in 2004 where he played in the club's Champions League run. But he moved on again at the end of that season joining Sporting Lisbon in Portugal.

Mauricio has been capped more than ten times by his country and was Chile's leading scorer in the World Cup 2006 Qualifying campaign netting three goals for his country.

Christos Karypidis

Greek defender Christos was signed in August 2006 after prolonged negotiations with PAOK Salonika in Greece where he began his career and came up through the youth system.

Born on December 2 1982 in Thessaloniki, Christos joined up with PAOK and got his break when he played his first professional match for the club in 2001. There followed a brief spell on loan to AO Kavala later that year and a second period away at AO Kerkyre in 2003. But Christos returned to PAOK for the 2003-04 season and went on to be part of the club's UEFA Cup squad in 2004 and again in 2005 when he lined up against Shakhtar Donetsk, VfB Stuttgart and Rapid Bucharest. His European experience will surely be useful to Hearts as they look to progress in Europe.

Christos has also played on the international stage featuring in the football tournament at the Olympic Games in Athens in 2004 for Greece.

Tiago Costa

Born on 22 April 1985, Tiago began his football career when he was signed at the age of ten to the Portuguese side Benfica, although he never made it to their first team. During Hearts' 2006/07 pre-season tour in Austria he played against Spartak Trnava and FC Cluj, and again against Berwick Rangers in the young Hearts team, before he signed a two-year deal at Tynecastle in August 2006. A talented and quick midfielder, the Portuguese player also works well in a right back position, and will provide competition for Robbie Neilson.

PLAYER QUIZ

1. Which lower division club did Robbie Neilson enjoy a spell on loan with?
2. Takis Fyssas has played in national cup finals in three different countries but for which clubs?
3. With which club did Paul Hartley start his career?
4. Against which club did Lee Wallace make his Hearts' debut?
5. For which Spanish club did Edgaras Jankauskas play?
6. On which ground did Craig Gordon make his Scotland international debut?
7. Which English club paid Rangers £630,000 to lure Steven Pressley south?
8. With which other club has Jose Goncalves played in the Champions League?
9. Who scored Hearts' first goal of the 2005-06 Premierleague campaign?
10. Who was the last player to find the net for Hearts during the 2005-06 season?
11. Name the four Hearts' players who were on target during the penalty shoot-out with Gretna at Hampden last May?
12. Which Gretna players missed during the cup final penalty shoot-out?
13. Which team did Roman Bednar help to the Czech Second Division title in 2003-04?
14. True or false – Paul Hartley scored from the penalty spot in all three of Hearts' wins over Hibs last season?
15. Who scored Hearts' first goal of 2006?
16. Against which team did Steve Banks make his first start for Hearts?
17. What do Paul Hartley and Walter Kidd have in common?
18. Who scored Hearts' first goal at Hampden last season?
19. Who was the first Hearts' player to be substituted last season?
20. Who was the last Hearts' player to be substituted last season?

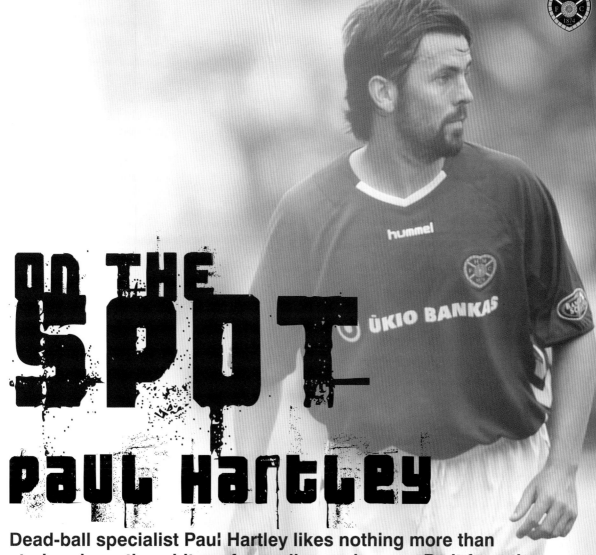

ON THE SPOT
PAUL HARTLEY

Dead-ball specialist Paul Hartley likes nothing more than staring down the whites of a goalkeeper's eyes. Be it from the penalty spot or from a free-kick outside the area, the midfield player can pick his spot with deadly accuracy. He may have missed out on the penalty shoot-out in the Scottish Cup final due to an ill-timed red card, but he has given Hearts fans plenty of moments to savour.

But, after the 2005-06 campaign literally went down to the last kick of the ball, here we look at some of Paul's set-pieces from last season.

July 30, 2005: Premier League: Kilmarnock 2 Hearts 4

The first day of the season and George Burley's debut match in charge. Much had been written about Hearts' new recruits but they had scarcely had time to gel before the trip to Ayrshire for what was always a difficult test. Hearts looked to be coasting at 3-1 but Gordon Greer pulled a goal back for Kilmarnock with just 16 minutes left to set up a grandstand finish. There were chances at both ends before one of the Hearts' newcomers Edgaras Jankauskas was fouled in the penalty area. Step forward Hartley who thrashed the ball past Alan Combe with conviction to signal three points and the first step on a remarkable season's journey. Hartley was to feature prominently throughout the season and scooped most of the player-of-the-year awards from supporters' clubs.

November 26, 2005: Premier League: Motherwell 1 Hearts 1

Graham Rix faced an early setback in his first away match as Hearts manager as his team toiled for long spells at Fir Park. Motherwell have proved sticky opposition in the past and looked set for all three points thanks to a first-half striker from Brian McLean. Hearts struggled to get out of third gear throughout a difficult contest but they were offered a lifeline in the first minute of injury-time when referee Iain Brines pointed to the penalty spot after Andy Webster had been fouled. It required nerves of steel and Hartley was the man to provide them as he slotted the penalty into the bottom corner of the net. It had not been convincing but it proved an invaluable goal as it kept Hearts in contention at the top with only one defeat in 16 league games.

January 28, 2006: Premier League: Hearts 4 Hibernian 1

Hearts were looking to slug it out toe-to-toe with Celtic for the Premier League title and the visit of neighbours Hibs gave them a difficult obstacle to overcome. Yet it was to prove to be one of Hearts' most comfortable wins of the season and Hartley chipped in with a double to ease his team to the three points. He opened the scoring from a Rudi Skacel pass after 27 minutes before Skacel himself added a second four minutes from the break. A minute from the break, the Czech was then felled by Gary Caldwell in the penalty box and it left Hartley with the chance to wrap up the points before the break. He did not disappoint as he lashed the penalty gleefully past Simon Brown to give Hearts a 3-0 half-time lead. Hearts eased off in the second half after Calum Elliot scored a fourth against ten-man Hibs who had Gary Smith sent off and Garry O'Connor pulled back a consolation goal.

February 7, 2006: Premier League: Dundee United 1 Hearts 1

This was a difficult match for Hearts. Pre-match speculation centred on who had picked the Hearts' team with Graham Rix suggesting that he had not had the final say. Such a revelation could not have helped the build-up to the game and it was hardly surprising that Hearts were a goal behind at half-time after Grant Brebner had put the home side ahead. Hearts, still relentlessly pursing Celtic and seeking to close the gap to three points with a win, stuck to their task and were given a break when they were awarded a penalty seven minutes from time after referee Dougie McDonald spotted an offence by Alan Archibald. As United fumed, their goalkeeper Derek Stillie was sent the wrong way with the spot-kick to salvage a point from a match that looked to be slipping away. Barry Robson and Julien Brellier were later red-carded as the game erupted in the final minutes.

April 2, 2006: Scottish Cup Semi Final: Hearts 4 Hibernian 0

Hartley settled the biggest Edinburgh derby in many years with a stunning hat-trick. But it was his second goal, from a free-kick after 59 minutes, which showed that he is a special player. Hearts were awarded a free-kick wide on the left after Takis Fyssas had been fouled. It looked as if Hartley would send a cross into the penalty area aimed at a team-mate but he had other ideas. He spotted Hibs' goalkeeper Zibi Malkowski had strayed from his line and left a gap at his near-post. It was all the encouragement he needed as he expertly squeezed the ball between the goalkeeper and post before Malkowski could react effectively and it was 2-0 to Hearts. It was a flash of genius that all but killed off Hibs and he completed his hat-trick from the penalty spot with two minutes remaining to cap a memorable day.

April 30, 2006: Premier League: Hearts 3 Celtic 0

Rangers were breathing heavily down Hearts' necks in the chase for the remaining Champions League place and were looking to arch-rivals Celtic to do them a favour. Celtic had already clinched the league but the Jambos knew that Gordon Strachan's side would not lie down. Leading by an early own goal from Stephen McManus, another piece of quick-thinking from Hartley put Hearts in full control in the ninth minute. Referee Alan Freeland awarded a free-kick outside the area after a clumsy challenge by Stan Varga on Roman Bednar. Hartley quickly grabbed the ball and, seeing that Celtic were loitering as they set up their defensive wall, he caught goalkeeper Artur Boruc off his guard by guiding a quickly-taken free-kick into the top corner of the net. Celtic were left stunned as referee Freeland signalled the goal and a second-half goal from Bednar gave the home side a comfortable win.

May 3, 2006: Premier League: Hearts 1 Aberdeen 0

Hartley kept his nerve as Hearts secured a Champions League place for a priceless goal. The home side had huffed and puffed their way through a nerve-ridden first half and it looked as if the goal they craved would never arrive.

Nine minutes into the second half, the breakthrough came. Russell Anderson handled the ball on his goal-line for an undisputed penalty. Hartley had to deal with the weight of expectation on his shoulders. But, such had been his consistency all season, few doubted where the ball was heading. The Scotland international kept his cool to send his kick beyond Jamie Langfield and into the net for the only goal of the game. The celebrations went long into the night.

HOME IS WHERE

Tynecastle has witnessed some glorious European nights. The 5-1 win over Lokomotiv Leipzig in 1976 and the 1-0 win over Bayern Munich in 1989 will live forever in the memory of Hearts' fans. Here we look at other European nights where the fans have raised the roof.

November 23, 1988: UEFA Cup, third round, first leg: Hearts 3 Velez Mostar 0

Over 17,000 packed Tynecastle in anticipation after Hearts had produced one of their finest displays in Europe in the previous round to see off Austria Vienna. Little was known about third round opponents Mostar but Yugoslavian football was respected throughout Europe and Hearts would have to overcome a difficult obstacle to progress to the last eight.

Although they had not won a league match for six weeks, Alex MacDonald's men were a different side in Europe that season and produced another stirring performance against their opponents. Hearts stamped their authority on the match from the outset and Iain Ferguson and John Colquhoun both came close before experienced European campaigner Eamonn Bannon opened the scoring after 19 minutes with a well-struck shot.

A mistake by the Mostar goalkeeper gave Mike Galloway the chance to make it 2-0 early in the second half and Hearts were well in control. Mostar's frustrations became obvious when star player Safet Susic was sent off for a bad tackle on Colquhoun to leave the visitors with ten men. Hearts took full advantage and Colqhoun added a third before the final whistle after Gary Mackay had set him up.

There was no doubt amongst the Hearts' fans at the final whistle that a quarter-final place had been booked but there was a difficult second leg in Mostar to negotiate in front of a hostile crowd. Hearts lost the return 2-1 but Galloway's away goal settled any concerns and they went through on a 4-2 aggregate to face Bayern Munich in the quarter-finals.

October 24, 1990: UEFA Cup, second round, first leg: Hearts 3 Bologna 1

One of Joe Jordan's first tests as Hearts manager pitted him against a team he was familiar with from his days as a player in Serie A.

Caretaker manager Sandy Clark had safely negotiated a hazardous first round trip to the Ukraine where Hearts drew 1-1 with Dnepr Dnepropetrovsk to set up a 3-1 home win in which John Robertson scored twice.

The draw against Bologna was much anticipated by players and management but the home gate of just over 11,000 for the first leg at Tynecastle was not as it should have been due to a decision to increase ticket prices significantly for the tie. It was 7,000 less than had witnessed the dismantling of Dnepr.

Hearts' form was patchy going into the fixture but the team raised their performance to produce a memorable European night.

With Robertson injured, Wayne Foster led the line and took just six minutes to slot home a left-foot shot. John Colquhoun then set up Foster's second goal and Bologna were close to collapse when Iain Ferguson headed a third goal seven minutes from half-time after his initial effort had come back off the crossbar.

But the Italians hit back in the second half and Hearts lost the away goal they had sought to avoid. Henry Smith was booked for time-wasting in the 61st minute and from the free-kick, Massimo Bonini rolled the ball to Egidio Notaristefano and the slammed the ball home.

Bologna were reduced to ten men moments later when Herbert Waas lashed out at Dave McPherson but Hearts could not make numerical advantage count in the closing stages. It was to prove costly as Bologna won the return leg a fortnight later 3-0 to go through on a 4-3 aggregate.

September 30, 1992: UEFA Cup, first round, second leg: Hearts 4 Slavia Prague 2

One of the classic European nights at Tynecastle as the home fans were put through a night of high anxiety but, ultimately, unfettered ecstasy. Hearts escaped from the first leg in Prague trailing just 1-0 against an impressive Slavia side as Henry Smith proved the hero of the tie with a number of fine saves.

Over 16,000 fans packed Tynecastle for the return and were rewarded with a cracking old-fashioned cup tie. Hearts wiped out Slavia's lead when Gary Mackay scored early in the game with a low shot but the Czechs hit back and Tomas Silhavy equalised midway through the first half. Ian Baird headed Hearts back in front after great work from Eamonn Bannon but Slavia still held the advantage on away goals.

Hearts needed a third to get through and, three minutes from half-time, Craig Levein – suspended for the first leg – supplied it with a rare goal as he headed in from a corner kick.

But it was not over yet. The tide looked to have turned Hearts' way when Penicka was sent off for a wild challenge on Baird but it seemed to work against the home side. Pavel Kuka pulled a goal back midway through the second half to make it 3-3 on aggregate and put the visitors back in the box seat.

Hearts stuck to the task and Glyn Snodin produced the winner with 11 minutes left with one of the best goals seen at Tynecastle. He looked over-ambitious as he lined up a free-kick 30 yards from goal but he found the top corner of the net for a thrilling strike which sent the Hearts' fans wild with delight.

Hearts held on to win 4-2 on the night and 4-3 on aggregate to book a second round place against FC Liege.

September 14, 1993: UEFA Cup, first round, first leg: Hearts 2 Atletico Madrid 1

Sandy Clark occupied the manager's chair after the departure of Joe Jordan and he had stamped his own mark on the team by bringing in Justin Fashanu, Jim Weir and Scott Leitch. Clark had been in interim charge three seasons previously when Hearts escaped with a 1-1 draw against Dnepr in the Ukraine and he relished the draw against the Spanish side.

Atletico had an impressive European pedigree but were perhaps best known in Scotland for a bad-tempered European Cup semi-final with Celtic in 1974 in Glasgow.

The Tynecastle tie – watched by a rain-soaked crowd of 15,596 - certainly had its share of wild challenges, particularly in a goalless first half, as the Spanish side sought to keep Hearts out at all costs.

They looked to have succeeded as Hearts looked to have become more frustrated as the game wore on. But John Robertson finally broke the deadlock with a typical poacher's finish after the Atletico goalkeeper had parried a Fashanu header.

John Colquhoun then added a second goal from a Gary Locke pass and Hearts were on the verge of one of their best results in Europe.

But a costly lapse in concentration at the back after 77 minutes gave Atletico an important away goal when Roman Kesecki shot past Henry Smith and it left Hearts with a difficult trip to Madrid.

Hearts did well enough in the return and the tie was level on aggregate going into the final 20 minutes with Hearts pressing for a goal.

But individual errors gifted Atletico two goals and they ran out 3-0 winners on the night to qualify on a 4-2 aggregate.

 September 14, 2000: UEFA Cup, first round, second leg: Hearts 3 Stuttgart 2

Hearts trailed 1-0 from the first leg in Germany but had high hopes of progressing against a young Stuttgart side. It was to prove a memorable, if ultimately frustrating, night at Tynecastle as Hearts came up short after a thrilling contest.

Steven Pressley levelled the scores on aggregate when he bundled the ball home at a corner in spite of being fouled and it set up a cracking tie in which the outcome was in doubt right up until the final whistle.

The goal meant Stuttgart could not sit in and they hit back with former Liverpool striker Sean Dundee netting an equaliser before the excellent Marcelo Bordon gave the Germans a 2-1 lead and a two-goal cushion on aggregate.

Hearts looked out of it but Gordan Petric equalised on the night to ensure it was an uncomfortable finale for the German side.

Hearts manager Jim Jefferies threw caution to the wind as he went for glory and the towering Kevin James was thrown into the attack which clearly unsettled the Stuttgart defence.

Colin Cameron made it 3-2 to Hearts by netting from the penalty spot in the closing stages and suddenly everyone inside Tynecastle suspected that a famous win was on the cards.

Stuttgart packed their defence in the final minutes to try and keep Hearts out but the home side sensed victory.

A golden chance fell to Petric right at the death when he was one-on-one with the goalkeeper but the defender rushed his effort and it flashed over the top and the final chance was gone.

Hearts went out on the away goals rule but the relief on the Stuttgart players' faces at the end spoke volumes for how close Jefferies' side had come.

Club Quiz

History

1. 1874.
2. Four – 1895, 1897, 1958 and 1960.
3. 21-0 v Anchor in October, 1880.
4. 1962 – with a 1-0 final win over Kilmarnock.
5. Red, white and blue.

Hearts' Greats

1. Barney Battles – 44 in 1930-31.
2. Gary Mackay (515).
3. Jimmy Wardhaugh – 376 in 519 matches in all competitions.
4. Three.
5. Tom Purdie.

Managers

1. Bobby Moncur.
2. Tommy Walker.
3. Davie McLean.
4. Joe Jordan.
5. Berwick Rangers.

Europe

1. Royal Standard Liege – in the European Cup in 1958.
2. Hamburg.
3. Iain Ferguson.
4. **Paris St Germain.**
5. Benfica – 1-2 in 1960.

Wordsearch

M	E	C	Y	R	R	E	B	K	G	I
S	X	L	E	S	S	B	E	E	O	N
E	Y	E	L	S	S	E	R	P	N	X
V	F	M	T	I	N	A	R	K	C	P
L	Y	C	R	J	O	L	A	N	G	R
A	S	C	A	M	A	T	S	O	E	R
C	S	T	H	C	H	Y	R	S	L	E
N	A	S	A	C	F	D	D	L	Q	B
O	S	L	R	A	O	E	A	I	S	N
G	E	E	T	N	B	T	Y	E	S	A
Y	L	N	U	N	B	E	D	N	A	R
X	L	G	O	R	D	L	Y	P	R	E

Player Quiz

1. Queen of the South.
2. Panionios AND Panathinaikos (Greece), Benfica (Portugal) and Hearts.
3. Hamilton.
4. Kilmarnock – in a Scottish Cup tie in February 2005.
5. Real Sociedad.
6. Easter Road – in a friendly against Trinidad & Tobago.
7. Coventry City.
8. FC Thun.
9. Rudi Skacel.
10. Michal Pospisil (in the Scottish Cup final penalty shoot-out).
11. Steven Pressley, Robbie Neilson, Rudi Skacel and Michal Pospisil.
12. Derek Townsley and Ryan Skelton.
13. Mlada Boleslav.
14. True – he scored six goals in all last season against the Easter Road side, three of which came from the spot.
15. Edgaras Jankauskas – against Celtic on New Year's Day at Tynecastle.
16. Celtic – in a 1-1 draw in Glasgow in October 2005.
17. Both have been sent off in Scottish Cup finals for Hearts.
18. Edgaras Jankauskas – in a 2-0 win over Queen's Park in a League Cup tie in August 2005.
19. Roman Bednar – replaced by Calum Elliot after 68 minutes of the opening league win at Kilmarnock.
20. Deividas Cesnauskas – replaced by compatriot Saulius Mikoliunas after 86 minutes of the Scottish Cup final.